How to Understand the Bible

Woodrow Kroll

BACK TO THE BIBLE
LINCOLN, NE 68501

Introduction

God wants you to know about yourself—your sin and your need for a Savior. He also wants you to know about Himself—His character, His hatred of sin and His deep love for you. He wants you to know of His plan for your future.

So He has recorded His Word, the Bible, for you to read, understand and obey.

God was the author of this book. He directed Moses, Paul, Peter, Daniel and others to write His words down. Their original writings were infallible, without error, and He preserved His Word through the ages. He watched over the copyists who, employing stringent procedures, made copies of the original writings.

The problem comes, however, when you pick up your Bible and start reading it. It must now filter through your understanding and interpretation—and they are not inspired. You certainly don't want to interpret what God said in a way that He didn't intend. How can you understand it, especially when it doesn't seem to make sense? How can you be sure you are interpreting it correctly? You need three things.

First, you need basic rules to help you interpret the Bible in a correct and meaningful way. That's what this book contains—12 maxims to help you make sense of, to interpret and to understand the Bible. If you follow them carefully and faithfully, you'll be able to better understand the Bible.

Second, you need God-given common sense. God wrote His Word for you—not just for scholars. The Bible makes sense, and you can understand it.

Third, you need time and effort. Understanding Scripture requires more than intellectual capacity. It takes commitment to God. Many Christians don't understand the Bible because they simply haven't tried hard enough. They've spent a little time in study, then they got bored or distracted. They put their Bibles away and still know little of what God wants them to know.

Make a commitment with God right now, or renew your commitment, to understand Him better by understanding His Word better. Set aside some time regularly to read His Word, meditate on it, memorize it and apply what you've read to your life. That's why He gave you the Bible. Take advantage of it.

Chapter 1

Begin With Prayer

Maxim 1: Begin with prayer and ask the Holy Spirit to be your interpreter and teacher.

When I study the Bible, I find a quiet spot and get alone. In my home that's in my study. There I can pray and seek help from God in interpreting His Word. Usually I pray for four things.

First, I pray for guidance. Your Bible study will be much more fruitful if you seek help from God. James said, "If any of you lacks wisdom, let him ask of God" (1:5). God never tires of our coming to Him for help. And it's much better for you to seek His help than to try to interpret Scripture on your own, for humans are prone to error. So ask for God's guidance; He will help you.

Second, I pray for truth. Jesus said, "And you shall know the truth, and the truth shall make you free" (John 8:32). But the truth is not always easily discerned. Sometimes we have a hard time finding it. You wouldn't want to pour over God's Word, prepare a Bible study, present it and then find out that what you said was not true. Our study of the Bible must lead us to the truth; so pray that God's truth, the main truth of the passage you are studying, will become evident to you.

Third, I pray for insight. Sometimes we can find the truth, but we don't have much insight into it. Insight is the power of seeing into a situation. It's the ability to comprehend the inner nature of something. People who have insight see beyond the truth—they see inside it. They get to the heart of a matter. They mine things from the truth that other people don't even see. Insight is a gift from God, and it can be yours. Ask the Spirit of God for insight as you study the Bible. Remember, "The Spirit searches all things, yes, the deep things of God" (1 Cor. 2:10). Ask Him to show you some of the deep things.

Fourth, I pray for application. Your understanding of the Word begins when you apply its truths to your life. Pray that the Spirit will make the truth you discover and the insight you receive intensely practical to you. Ask Him to show you a situation today in which you can apply a truth you have learned from the Bible.

To get the most out of your Bible study, don't try it alone. You can have the help of a great teacher—the Master Teacher. Jesus said, "The Holy Spirit . . . will teach you all things" (John 14:26). Begin with prayer and ask the Holy Spirit to be your interpreter and teacher.

Chapter 2

The Bible Is Literal

Maxim 2: Generally, the Bible should be interpreted literally, exactly as it is written.

Note that maxim 2 uses the word *generally*. The Bible, like any other book, uses figures of speech, and these require different rules of interpretation.

For example, have you ever said, "I'm so hungry I could eat a horse"? We call that hyperbole. You really can't eat a horse, and if you could, why would you want to? No, that exaggeration is said for effect and is not meant literally.

The Bible occasionally uses hyperbole too. John said, "And there are also many other things that Jesus did, which if they were written one by one, I suppose that even the world itself could not contain the books that would be written" (John 21:25). Of course, John simply meant that Jesus did many other things that the apostle did not record.

The Bible uses other figures of speech, including similes and metaphors. A simile makes a comparison by using the word *like* or *as*. Solomon said to his beloved, "Your teeth are like a flock of shorn sheep" (Song of Sol. 4:2). That doesn't sound very complimentary. But he meant it as a compliment. He was saying that the teeth of his beloved are white and smooth, like a shorn sheep.

A metaphor also makes a comparison, but it omits the comparative word. Solomon complimented his beloved by telling her, "Your navel is a rounded goblet" (Song of Sol. 7:2). Obviously, Solomon's reference to a flock of shorn sheep or a rounded goblet was not meant to be taken literally. He used these figures of speech to describe something that was literal.

God knew what He wanted to say in the Scriptures. We should trust that He said what He meant. You should always attempt to interpret Scripture literally, unless a literal interpretation doesn't make good sense. Here's a good rule to follow: "When the plain sense of Scripture makes common sense, seek no other sense."[1]

God wants you to understand your Bible, and you can. Take every word to mean what you ordinarily would think it means, unless the facts or the immediate context indicate otherwise. No other interpretation does justice to God's desire for you to know what's on His mind.

And if you find passages that cannot be taken literally, take them in stride. They may be parables. Jesus was fond of using parables—stories that easily could have happened but didn't—to teach things that clearly did happen. The parable of the Prodigal Son is an excellent example. Through it Jesus wanted to teach us about attitudes toward one another, so He told a story that was plausible, even though it was not historical.

When you interpret prophetic or apocalyptic passages, such as those in the Book of Revelation, you will notice that many things don't seem to make sense if they are taken literally. In that case, treat the passages figuratively.

Follow the rules of biblical interpretation, and you'll be surprised how much you can understand on your own.

[1] Cooper, David L., *What Men Must Believe*, Los Angeles: Biblical Research Society, 1943, p. 63.

Chapter 3

A Progressive Revelation

Maxim 3: Interpret the Bible as a progressive revelation of God.

I enjoy Agatha Christie's mysteries. She reveals clues in such a way that, right to the end, I'm never quite sure who the villain is. If I make a judgment too early, I'm likely disappointed at the end of the book. It's necessary to follow the progressive unfolding of the story before drawing conclusions.

God is much more skilled at revelation than the most popular mystery writer. But just as when we read a good mystery, we must be careful not to base our conclusions on early information alone when we interpret the Bible.

God revealed His Word over a period of many centuries; that is called progressive revelation. Everything He said was true, but He didn't say everything at once.

From all eternity God has been and is the omniscient, the all-knowing God. When He revealed His Word to Moses, He knew everything, but He didn't choose to reveal everything to Moses. He chose to reveal some of these things centuries later—some to Paul and others to John.

11

God revealed things to the prophets that were unknown to those who preceded them. And He gave wisdom to the apostles and New Testament writers that He kept from the Old Testament writers.

The more God revealed, the more men understood. Even today we don't understand everything He revealed in His Word, but one day we will. "For now we see in a mirror, dimly, but then face to face" (1 Cor. 13:12).

Three things will help us understand how God revealed Himself progressively.

Genesis is the acorn; the Bible is the tree

Just as the acorn contains in rudimentary form all that an oak tree contains, so the Book of Genesis contains in rudimentary form almost all that the Bible contains.

Genesis is called the "Book of Beginnings," but it's more. It's like an acorn that gives rise to the full revelation of God. Everything that God deemed spiritually and morally important for us to know is found in the Bible. And those truths are found in their kernel form in Genesis.

Genesis contains heaven's official explanation of the origin of all things: "In the beginning God created the heavens and the earth" (1:1). It shows the establishment of God's plan for male and female relationships and ultimately the ideal for marriage: "A man shall leave his father and mother and be joined to his wife, and they shall become one flesh" (2:24). The foundation of society is found in Genesis (4:17), as well as some of the rules for governing society (9:6). The origin of man's sin is recorded in Genesis (3:6), as well as God's first revelation of how He would redeem mankind (3:15).

The first book of the Bible contains foundational truth, but we cannot fully appreciate the beauty of the oak tree by looking at the acorn. We need to see the development of the tree. We need more than the Book of Genesis to understand the mind of God. So God continued to reveal Himself to us throughout the Old Testament.

The Old Testament is largely foundational truth

If you didn't know anything about God, where would you begin your study about Him? If you said the Gospel of John or the New Testament, I disagree. You get a well-rounded picture of God only if you start in the Old Testament. The New Testament depicts God as the loving Heavenly Father, the God who loved you so much that He sent His Son to die for you. That's the kind of God we like to hear about, but that understanding is not complete.

Just as the Book of Genesis contains rudimentary elements of the rest of the Bible, the Old Testament contains foundational truth that you have to understand before you can appreciate the New Testament fully.

In Genesis we get a picture of Jehovah as a God with clearly defined standards. He expects His creation to respect those standards. When Adam and Eve didn't, God revealed that He keeps His word by punishing them for their sin (Gen. 3). Still, He showed that He loves those who sin against Him, and He provided for Adam and Eve (3:21). He did the same for Cain (4:15) and for others.

But we can't come to a full appreciation of God's character until we read further in the Old Testament.

In Exodus we learn that God is serious about His standards, as codified in the Ten Commandments. In Leviticus, Numbers and Deuteronomy, we learn more of how God responds to those who break His commandments. But we also learn more of His grace in the midst of punishment.

God progressively revealed Himself to His people throughout the Old Testament, and His people progressively understood His character better. That revelation didn't end with the Old Testament but continued into the New.

The New Testament is largely fulfilled truth

Much of what we learn of God from the Old Testament needs additional explanation. The New Testament helps explain what we cannot understand in the Old.

With the birth of Jesus Christ, the promises of the Old Testament take on new meaning. And they help us understand what God's dealings with Israel were all about.

The New Testament teaches us that Jesus is the fulfillment of much of what we read in the Old Testament. Jesus said, "Do not think that I came to destroy the Law or the Prophets. I did not come to destroy but to fulfill" (Matt. 5:17). Paul said, "For Christ is the end of the law for righteousness to everyone who believes" (Rom. 10:4).

Jesus did not nullify the Law or the Prophets; He did what no one in the Old Testament ever could do—He kept all the Law. He alone obeyed it completely. He gave real meaning to the prophecies of the Old Testament, for many of them were about Him. His birth, life, death and Resurrection proved that the Old Testament prophets had truly received a message from God.

The foundational truth of the Old Testament flowers into fulfilled truth in the New Testament, just as the acorn of Genesis grew into the tall oak of the Bible. But what does this have to do with your interpreting the Bible correctly? A great deal.

If you want the full truth, you have to interpret the earlier passages of Scripture in light of later passages. You need to apply what you have learned in the Gospels and the epistles to your interpretation of the Old Testament.

Chapter 4

No Contradictions

Maxim 4: Never interpret a text in a way that contradicts the rest of Scripture.

It stands to reason that you should never interpret a text in a way that contradicts other passages of the Bible. But people commonly make that mistake. They see a verse that appears to contradict what other verses say, and they are baffled. So they jump to the conclusion that there must be a contradiction in the Bible.

When you find something in your Bible study that doesn't make sense, that seems to be saying the opposite of what you've read elsewhere, you can assume that there is a reasonable explanation. Remember that just because you don't have an explanation for such a problem doesn't mean that none exists.

We must assume that any apparent contradiction in the Bible results from our improper interpretation of the text, not from a contradiction in God's thinking.

Here are two examples of texts that challenge our interpretive skills. One is from the Old Testament; the other is from the New. Each shows us that we must never interpret a text in a way that contradicts the rest of Scripture.

The example of Psalm 44

Psalm 121: 3–4 says of God, "He who keeps you will not slumber. Behold, He who keeps Israel shall neither slumber nor sleep."

But in Psalm 44:23 the sons of Korah said, "Awake! Why do You sleep, O Lord? Arise! Do not cast us off forever." Doesn't this contradict what other verses in the Bible have said about God?

We know that God doesn't sleep. When Elijah was on Mount Carmel challenging the prophets of Baal because their god didn't answer by fire, he suggested, "Perhaps he is sleeping and must be awakened" (1 Kings 18:27). Suggesting that Baal was asleep is one thing. But if Jehovah had been sleeping, there would have been no flash fire to consume the sacrifice that day.

What did the sons of Korah mean? How should we understand this challenge to God?

Psalm 44 has nothing to do with the idea that God might be sleeping. Instead, it reflects Israel's search for answers after it suffered military defeats. The Jews knew that Jehovah was their God, but they lost the battle anyway. The sons of Korah were not trying to rouse Him from sleep. They were calling on Him to come to their aid, to champion the cause of His people. Their prayer was couched in military terms.

Had we assumed that Psalm 44 contradicted all other Scriptures that say God never sleeps, we would have been disappointed—and in serious error. We are never at liberty to interpret a passage in a way that contradicts the rest of Scripture. And when we look for an interpretation that is consistent with the rest of

God's Word, the Spirit of God will show us one; and it will be the right one.

The example of Philippians 2

There is one verse that I am frequently asked about—Philippians 2:12. It says, "Work out your own salvation with fear and trembling." People sometimes think this means that we have to *work for* our salvation.

But the Bible clearly teaches that our salvation is by faith alone. It's the work of God from beginning to end. He inaugurated it, maintains it and will complete it. You have His word on that (Phil. 1:6).

No one can work for salvation. Many passages teach us this truth, including Acts 16:31, Titus 3:5 and especially Ephesians 2:8–9, which says, "For by grace you have been saved through faith, and that not of yourselves; it is the gift of God, not of works, lest anyone should boast."

But verse 10 of Ephesians 2 should not be forgotten. It says, "For we are His workmanship, created in Christ Jesus for good works, which God prepared beforehand that we should walk in them."

Our good works could never be good enough for God to accept in atonement for our sin. That's why we must look to Him and His grace alone for salvation.

But when God saved us, it was for a purpose, and that purpose is to work for Him, to accomplish His will. That's what Paul meant when he said, "Work out your own salvation." He didn't mean that we should work *toward* salvation. Rather, we are to work

God's salvation *out* through the way we live and the way we serve Him.

There's no contradiction in these verses as long as we interpret them correctly.

How can you be sure that you are interpreting a passage correctly if it seems to contradict another passage? Here are three suggestions.

1. Look for additional Scriptures that might shed light on the passage that puzzles you.

2. Consider who is speaking when you interpret a text. For example, Job's friends were not speaking for God. So if they contradicted the plain teaching of Scripture when they spoke to Job, you should not be surprised.

3. Adopt the interpretation that most closely aligns itself with God's character.

When you search the Scriptures and cannot find other verses that will help you interpret the verse in question, ask yourself, Which interpretation best reflects what the Bible teaches about the character and purpose of God?

We must not interpret a passage in a way that closely fits our thinking, our biases and our wishes while we ignore the interpretation that most closely fits the rest of God's Word.

Chapter 5

Context Is Key

Maxim 5: Interpret a text in light of its immediate context.

This maxim is not just a play on the words *text* and *context*. It has real meaning. In fact, it's one of your most important helps for interpreting Scripture.

What does *context* mean? Webster's Dictionary defines it as "the parts of a discourse that surround a word or passage and can throw light on its meaning."

If you study the context of a passage, you will find help in understanding the passage itself. Never interpret a text in a way that is not supported by its immediate context.

There are three things to remember about interpreting Scripture in the light of its context.

1. Context is a better interpreter than the most skillful commentator.

When you are studying the Bible and need help, don't reach for your favorite commentary first. If you do, you'll be cheating yourself. You'll not be giving yourself the opportunity to learn great truths from the context of the passage. And in the process you'll not be giving the Holy Spirit an opportunity to be your personal teacher. You can learn much more about the meaning of a text by reading the context than you can from reading your favorite commentary.

2. Context is a better teacher than the most skilled mentor.

Unless you are an old hand at interpreting the Bible, you may be puzzled about how to begin. What do you look for? What questions do you ask? You could go to a skilled teacher for help, or you could consult the context of a passage. The latter is the better choice, because the context is a better teacher than the most skilled mentor.

The immediate context—the verses or chapters just before or after the passage you want to interpret— will teach you what to look for. Ask some simple questions of the context, like these:

What was the writer talking about just before he mentioned the verse I am studying?

What is the whole chapter about?

What is this book of the Bible about?

Has the writer mentioned the topic of this verse previously in his book?

The answers to such questions will help you understand a tremendous amount about the text.

3. Context is a better protector than the most skilled defender.

You may have read someone's interpretation of a verse and thought, *This writer is really off the wall!* It's not difficult for people to devise some unusual interpretations of God's Word.

Sometimes I receive unsolicited literature from well-meaning people who have come to a particular interpretation of the Bible that no one else shares. After reading it, I often scratch my head and say, "How did they ever came up with this interpretation?"

There's a great way to protect yourself from the danger of such wacky interpretations. Let the context prevent you from interpreting a verse in a way that the writer of Scripture never intended.

For example, 1 Corinthians 15:31 says, "I die daily." What does it mean? Most people think it means that they die spiritually to self daily.

But the verse is a part of the great resurrection chapter. Verse 42 says, "The body is sown in corruption, it is raised in incorruption," and verses 56–57 say, "The sting of death is sin, and the strength of sin is the law. But thanks be to God, who gives us the victory through our Lord Jesus Christ." What powerful assurance! God will not leave our bodies in the grave but will one day raise us with a new and glorious body.

Just before Paul said, "I die daily," he mentioned putting his life on the line every day. Just after those three words, he spoke about fighting with wild beasts in the arena of Ephesus.

Do you think that Paul, in the middle of a discussion about death and the bodily resurrection, would dramatically shift gears and drop in three little words about dying spiritually to self? Obviously not. The context makes it clear that he is speaking of physical hardships, not dying to self spiritually.

We must never violate this maxim for interpretation: Interpret the Bible in light of its immediate context. The context is your interpreter, teacher and protector.

Chapter 6

Get Inside the Writer's Mind

Maxim 6: Interpret the Bible in light of its background.

The background of a passage differs from its context. The context includes the verses that are before and after the text. The background relates to all those things that help you get inside the writer's mind. They include his purpose for writing and any historical, geographical or cultural data that bears on the passage.

The purpose of writing

The writers of books of the Bible sometimes identified why they wrote. For example, John said, "And truly Jesus did many other signs in the presence of His disciples, which are not written in this book; but these are written that you may believe that Jesus is the Christ, the Son of God, and that believing you may have life in His name" (John 20:30–31).

This passage tells us that John wrote his Gospel to show us that Jesus is the Messiah and that through faith in Him we can have eternal life. When you understand John's purpose, you will understand how to interpret his book.

Other examples are found in 1 John: "And these things we write to you that your joy may be full" (1:4). John gave another reason for writing the book: "My little children, these things I write to you, that you may not sin" (2:1). He continues in chapter 2 to state his purpose for writing to little children in the faith (v. 12), to fathers and to young men (v. 13).

Historical background

Understanding the historical background of a Bible character or event will help you interpret the Bible. Herod, the king who killed innocent children when Jesus was a baby, is a good example. Matthew 2:16 says, "Then Herod, when he saw that he was deceived by the wise men, was exceedingly angry; and he sent forth and put to death all the male children who were in Bethlehem and in all its districts, from two years old and under, according to the time which he had determined from the wise men."

It is difficult to understand how a man could be so ruthless that he would murder babies. But if you understand something about Herod as a person, you won't have any difficulty understanding his cruelty.

Herod became known as "the Great" because of his renowned building activities. He constructed many cities throughout Palestine. But he was also a man of violence. He came to power at age 15. He had 10 wives, 2 of whom were his nieces. His wives and children plotted against each other. He had three of his sons killed (ages 9, 10 and 11), together with the mother of the two older sons. This was the legacy of the man who attempted to destroy Jesus by killing the babies of Bethlehem.

Geographical background

Christians know far too little about the geography of the Bible lands. If we understood the geography of the Bible better, we would understand the Bible much better too.

Someone once asked me, "How could it be that Jesus heard Peter's great confession of faith at Caesarea Philippi, when Philippi was located in Greece and Jesus never left Palestine?" This man did not understand that Caesarea Philippi and Caesarea were in Palestine, but Philippi was in Greece. Had he known more about geography, he would have understood the text better.

A classic example of the importance of knowing Bible geography is Jesus' story of the Good Samaritan. Luke 10:30–37 tells of a man who went down from Jerusalem to Jericho and fell among thieves. He was robbed, beaten and bloodied. But a good Samaritan found him and helped him.

People have been puzzled because the Bible says that he went *down* from Jerusalem to Jericho. Usually we speak of *down* as indicating south. But Jericho is 17 miles northeast of Jerusalem.

This can be explained easily when you understand the geography of the region. Jerusalem is 2,700 feet above sea level; Jericho is 700 feet below. Jerusalem is on the mountains, while Jericho is down in the Jordan Valley. The road from Jerusalem to Jericho, with a distance of only 17 miles, descends rapidly. Luke was correct to use the word *down*.

Cultural background

Understanding the cultural background of incidents in the Bible is also helpful in interpretation. Here is an example: At Caesarea Philippi Jesus said to Peter, "On this rock I will build My church, and the gates of Hades [hell] shall not prevail against it'" (Matt. 16:18).

How can gates prevail? Do gates attack an army, or does an army attack gates? What is the meaning of "the gates of hell?"

The answers to these questions involve culture. Gates were more than just a hole in a wall. They designated the seat of authority for a city. That's where men of renown sat and discussed things that pertained to the welfare of their city. Our present equivalent would be a government or parliament building. (If you visit Jerusalem and see the Golden Gate, you will notice that inside of the gate is a huge building.)

When Jesus said that the gates of hell will not prevail against the church, He was not talking about gates but about the authorities of hell, those who possess the wisdom of hell and make the decisions of hell. Satan and his demons will never prevail against Christ's Church.

Many biblical passages speak of cultural customs. Our struggle is to discern which of those practices are cultural and which are applicable today and thus transcend all cultural boundaries.

For example, the holy kiss may be cultural. But the Christian love we should have for one another in the body of Christ is transcultural. We may or may not kiss, but we must love all others in the church.

Additional cultural issues include the washing of feet, women covering their heads in church, standing to read the Scriptures and elements in the order of the worship service. In fact, decisions must be made concerning a great deal of church practice and polity. About each issue we must ask, Was it based only on culture? Or was it designed to be used forever?

Chapter 7

Watch the Grammar

Maxim 7: Pay close attention to grammatical constructions when you interpret the Bible.

Many students try to avoid grammar when they are in school. But an understanding of grammar is helpful in Bible study. There are some critically important aspects of grammar that we should focus on.

Meaning of verbs

First, you need to be aware of differences in the meanings of certain verbs.

One good example is found in Romans 1:1-4: "Paul, a servant of Jesus Christ, called to be an apostle, separated to the gospel of God which He promised before through the prophets in the Holy Scriptures, concerning His Son Jesus Christ our Lord, who was born of the seed of David according to the flesh, and declared to be the Son of God with power, according to the Spirit of holiness."

In this passage Paul changed verbs when he refered to Jesus. First he said that Jesus was *born* the seed of David. There was a time when Jesus was not the son of David, when He was not in flesh. That was before the virgin birth.

Later Paul said that Jesus was *declared* to be the Son of God. There was never a time when Jesus was not the Son of God. So the writer does not say that He was born the Son of God. He was simply *declared* to be God's Son. You cannot make someone become something he already is.

Pay attention to the verbs, especially the action verbs. Pay close attention when a Bible writer changes a verb.

Prepositions

Also note the parts of speech, especially prepositions. For example, in Romans 3:21–22 we read: "But now the righteousness of God apart from the law is revealed, being witnessed by the Law and the Prophets, even the righteousness of God which is through faith in Jesus Christ to all and on all who believe.

Notice the writer changed the preposition from *to* to *on*. He said that the righteousness of God that comes through faith in Jesus Christ is *to* all—but *on* only those who believe. This means that everyone has the possibility of having the righteousness of God applied to his life. But unless a person trusts Jesus Christ as Savior, this righteousness will never be applied to his account. That's the difference between "to all" and "on all."

Be cautious when you study your Bible. When translators produced English versions, they sometimes took liberties in their use of prepositions. If you find that a preposition is a crucial part of your interpretation of a passage, make sure that the English preposition means exactly the same as its counterpart in the original language.

You may have to ask your pastor or call a theology department of a Bible college. Or if you are studying the New Testament, you can buy any one of a number of Greek study aids for people who read English but not Greek.

Tenses of verbs

In John 14 Jesus comforted His disciples, assuring them that even though He must leave them, He would not leave them forever: "Let not your heart be troubled; you believe in God, believe also in Me. In My Father's house are many mansions; if it were not so, I would have told you. I go to prepare a place for you, and if I go and prepare a place for you, I will come again and receive you to Myself; that where I am there you may be also" (vv. 1–3).

There is an obvious change of tense in the verbs used in this passage. He said, "I go" and "I will come." Jesus has now gone, but one day He will come again for us. That's God's promise to you. Pay close attention to all the "will" and "shall" promises of the Bible; because if they have not already been fulfilled, you know that one day they will be.

References to time and place

In the Bible you find many references to time and place. Paying close attention to these references will help you understand Scripture.

John recorded the travels of the Lord Jesus, and he was careful to include many references to time and place. Here are some examples from his Gospel.

John 1:28: Jesus was baptized at Bethabara in the Jordan River, in Judea, in the southern part of Palestine.

John 1:43: Jesus went to Galilee, in the northern part of Palestine. There He called His disciples.

John 2:1: Jesus attended a wedding in Cana of Galilee.

John 2:12: Jesus moved on to Capernaum, but He did not stay there many days.

John 2:13: Jesus traveled south to Jerusalem at the Passover.

John 3:22: Jesus found His way to the Jordan River again.

John 4:3: Jesus left Judea and departed again for Galilee. But in order to get there, He had to go through Samaria. There He met the woman at the well.

John 4:43: After two days Jesus departed again for Galilee.

John 5:1: Jesus left Galilee and went south to Jerusalem for a feast of the Jews. There He healed the man at the Pool of Bethesda.

John 6:1: From there Jesus went over the Sea of Galilee, where He fed 5,000 people.

The first words of John 6:1 are "After these things." Any good interpreter of the Bible must ask himself: After what things? Why does John include this time reference? We've just looked at Jesus' travels, as recorded in the first five chapters of John, so we understand what "these things" are.

John was very good at giving time and place references, and this helps us interpret the Bible correctly.

Chapter 8

Let Scripture Interpret Scripture

Maxim 8: Take advantage of Scripture's interpretation of itself.

Frequently the Bible will answer your questions if you simply look for the answers there. Let the Bible be your guide in biblical interpretation.

John 6:1–5 says that Jesus was with a great multitude, and He asked Philip where they could get bread to feed them.

I've read many commentaries that speculate on why Jesus asked Philip this question. Some say that Philip was standing next to Him. Some say that Philip was cool and calculating. Some say that Philip lived in Bethsaida, which was nearby, and he would know where to find food.

But you don't have to spend time on foolish speculations like that, because the next verse explains why Jesus asked Philip this question: "But this He said to test him, for He Himself knew what He would do" (v. 6).

God wants you to understand your Bible. He has given you many clues in Scripture to help you. Look for those clues.

When Jesus healed a blind man and the man's parents refused to admit to the Pharisees that their son was healed by Jesus, John 9:22 explains that the parents did not want to be excommunicated from the synagogue. If you had read up to verse 21 and were amazed that the man's parents wouldn't corroborate his story, you would be helped by one of the most basic of all rules for Bible interpretation: Read a little further.

The most important ingredient in understanding the Bible is to spend enough time reading and studying it. When you do, you will realize that it is much easier to understand than you thought.

Set aside some time—sufficient, quality time—to read and think about the Word. When you do this consistently, day after day, you may even surprise yourself at what an adept interpreter of the Bible you have become.

Chapter 9

Rightly Divide the Word

Maxim 9: Proper interpretation requires that the Bible be rightly divided.

Second Timothy 2:15 says, "Be diligent to present yourself approved to God, a worker who does not need to be ashamed, rightly dividing the word of truth."

Be diligent in the New King James Version (*study* in the King James Version) means "endeavor" or "exert yourself" or "labor." Paul said that we should endeavor to be diligent in three areas:

1. We should endeavor to be an approved worker for God. The word *approved* means "accepted, proven trustworthy, full of integrity."

2. We should endeavor to be an unashamed worker for God. We ought to do everything we can so that we will not be ashamed of what we've done or make God ashamed of us.

3. We should endeavor to be a correctly informed worker for God. To do that, we must interpret the Bible correctly.

The word translated "rightly dividing" is the Greek word *orthotomeo,* meaning "to cut a straight line, to hold course, to handle rightly." The first part of the word, *ortho,* is used in the word *orthodontist,* a dentist who straightens teeth. Another kind of worker, a diamond cutter, looks at a diamond in the rough and sees how to cut a straight line to make a proper facet.

Paul wanted us to know that to interpret God's Word correctly, we have to handle it correctly. If God makes distinctions between things, we must also make proper distinctions between them. If we fail to see the distinctions God has made in His Word, we will fail to understand His Word correctly.

The Law and grace

For example, we must be aware that God draws distinctions between the Law and grace.

The Old Testament Law came as a result of the Mosaic Covenant, made between God and the people of Israel. Exodus 19:3 says, "And Moses went up to God, and the LORD called to him from the mountain, saying, 'Thus you shall say to the house of Jacob, and tell the children of Israel.'" It's evident that what follows—the Ten Commandments—were given by God to His people Israel.

While the Law is right and valuable and a proper guide for the morality of any people, we must remember that the Law was given to and for the chosen people of God—Israel.

Grace, on the other hand, is an attitude and action of God that cuts across racial and ethnic lines. The grace of God has appeared to all men, the Bible says. Grace is vastly different from the Law. In the Old Testament economy men and women lived under law; in the New Testament economy we live under grace.

John demonstrated how the distinction between the two should be perceived. He said, "For the law was given through Moses, but grace and truth came through Jesus Christ" (John 1:17).

No one has ever been saved by keeping the Law, because it has no power to save anyone. Even people in the Old Testament were saved by God's grace. They looked forward to the promises of God. They believed those promises, and in believing, they were saved.

Here's how Paul said it: "Therefore by the deeds of the law no flesh will be justified in His sight, for by the law is the knowledge of sin. But now the righteousness of God apart from the law is revealed, being witnessed by the Law and the Prophets, even the righteousness of God which is through faith in Jesus Christ to all and on all who believe. For there is no difference; for all have sinned and fall short of the glory of God, being justified freely by His grace through the redemption that is in Christ Jesus" (Rom. 3:20–24).

The Law is our teacher, our schoolmaster. It shows us how desperately we need the grace of God. But you are not saved by keeping the Ten Commandments. You are saved only by trusting in the finished work of Jesus Christ on the cross of Calvary. You must rightly divide the Word here or miss God's way of salvation. Make a distinction between the Law and grace.

Salvation and rewards

God also draws distinctions between salvation and rewards. Salvation is not earned—it's God's free gift. Rewards, on the other hand, are earned. They're not free.

There's nothing you can do to earn God's salvation. You can only thankfully receive it. Romans 6:23 says, "For the wages of sin is death, but the gift of God is eternal life in Christ Jesus our Lord."

But once you are saved, God expects you to earn the rewards that He will give you. That's the work that you do for Him. Ephesians 2:10 says, "We are . . . created in Christ Jesus [that's another way of saying we're saved] for good works, which God prepared beforehand that we should walk in them."

Israel and the Church

God also draws distinctions between Israel and the Church.

The people of God in the Old Testament were a chosen nation—Israel. They were a covenant people, a people whom God chose out of the rest of the nations to demonstrate to the world His purposes in salvation.

As a New Testament believer, I cannot claim many of the promises that God made to Israel. For example, God promised His people through Abraham that they would have a land filled with milk and honey for an everlasting possession. He said to Abraham, "Lift your eyes now and look . . . for all the land which you see I give to you and your descendants forever" (Gen. 13:14–15). I am not a descendent of Abraham; therefore, I can't claim that promise. The land is not mine.

God also promised Abraham a numerous, invincible, noble posterity through Sarah and Isaac. He also promised a posterity through Hagar and Ishmael. But the people of God would be born through Isaac (Gen.

17:19). I was not descended from Abraham through Isaac. So this promise was not made to me.

God dealt bountifully with His people Israel, but they rejected the only Messiah and Savior God will ever give them. They refused to see Jesus of Nazareth as the blessed seed of Abraham. Their spiritual blindness to Christ opened the door for God to shower His grace on Gentiles.

I'm grateful that He did, because as a Gentile believer, I am one of the elect people that God saved out of every tribe, nation and race. I am a part of the Church of God.

Paul said, "Give no offense, either to the Jews or to the Greeks or to the church of God" (1 Cor. 10:32). The Jews were God's chosen people. The Gentiles were everybody else. But the Church of God today is made up of Jews and Gentiles.

If you want to interpret your Bible in the way God wrote it, you must make the distinctions that God made and not blur those distinctions. Otherwise, you will be making claims that God never intended, exercising rules that He did not give to you and claiming promises He did not make to you.

Chapter 10

Interpretation vs. Application

Maxim 10: Bible interpretation is singular; Bible application may be plural.

God wrote each passage of the Bible, and He predetermined the one and only original interpretation of each passage.

While there is only one interpretation of a passage, however, you and I can apply what God said in many ways. That process is called application. Do not confuse it with interpretation.

For example, there is only one proper interpretation of Ezekiel 37:1–14, the passage concerning the vision of the Valley of Dry Bones. God wanted Ezekiel to understand that this prophecy was about Israel, the people of God. They had been dispersed throughout the Gentile nations. And one day He would draw them from the four corners of the earth and take them back to the homeland that He promised to their father Abraham and his seed.

But the application is a different matter. This passage may be applied in a variety of ways.

For example, it could be used as an illustration of new life in Christ. Ephesians 2:1 says that before we knew Christ as our Savior, we were dead in our trespasses and sins. We could do nothing to earn our salvation, for nothing we did was spiritually acceptable to God. We were spiritually dead.

But God breathed new life into us. In His marvelous grace He drew us to Himself and applied the blood of Jesus Christ to us. We who were dead have received new life in Christ. And that new life is akin to the life God will bring when He gathers up those old, dead bones and brings the nation of Israel back to life.

We must never interpret Ezekiel 37 to mean the salvation of all mankind. That's not the proper interpretation. But we may use this passage to illustrate how we receive new life in Christ. In so doing, we must keep this application separate from the one and only interpretation that was designed by God. Remember, interpretation is singular; Bible application may be plural.

Chapter 11

Get a Second Opinion

Maxim 11: After you have arrived at an interpretation, check it with others you trust.

After you have studied a passage in God's Word and think you know what it means, check with somebody else to see if you have the right interpretation.

Why? To avoid coming up with a wacky interpretation. Sometimes when we interpret the Bible all by ourselves, we have no system of checks and balances to insure that we are not in error. We need someone else to compare our ideas with.

Who should that person be? Someone you can trust to interpret the Bible correctly.

It might be your pastor. Say to him, "Pastor, I've been studying this portion of Scripture. This is what I think it means. What do you think? How would you modify my thoughts?" Or you might ask these questions of one of your teachers, a mentor or someone who has been discipling you.

Or you might read some Bible commentaries. If you are uncertain which ones you can trust and are unfamiliar with the authors, check on the publishers. Some of them can be trusted to print only what is consistent with the Word of God. Ask your pastor for advice, or write to us here at Back to the Bible. We will help you.

Don't be a lone interpreter of the Bible. Share your thinking with others whom you trust. Get their reaction. They may add something you never thought of, or they may point out some flaw in your interpretation.

Chapter 12

Be Charitable in Disagreements

Maxim 12: Always be charitable to those who differ with your interpretation.

We are all members in the same body, the Body of Christ. Each member has a different function, and that means that each member has a different perspective on the Body. The foot has a significant amount of weight put on it. But there's not much weight put on the finger—unless you're doing handstands.

Let's remember that Christians differ. Some are preoccupied with one doctrine or another. They eat, drink, sleep and breath the sovereignty of God or the necessity for evangelism or the propriety of using one translation of the Bible over another.

Let's be kind to one another when discussing our differences. Christians who differ in opinion from you are not the enemy; they are brothers and sisters in Christ, members of the same body. The enemy is Satan.

Interpret the Bible the way you think God meant it to be interpreted. Hold your beliefs with confidence. But always remember to be charitable to those who differ with your interpretation. After all, they may be right.

Back to the Bible is a nonprofit ministry dedicated to Bible teaching, evangelism and edification of Christians worldwide.

If we may assist you in knowing more about Christ and the Christian life, please write to us without obligation.

Back to the Bible
P.O. Box 82808
Lincoln, NE 68501